30 DEVOTIONS FOR FAITH THAT MOVES MOUNTAINS

PERSEVERANCE

A DEVOTABLE COMPILATION PROJECT

HARRIS
Author Services

CONTENTS

Acknowledgements

To my wife, kids, family, and friends; thank you for all the encouragement to pursue my passion and create something that not only helps me, but also helps others. Thank you for sacrificing your time with me so I could create something wonderful.

Thank you to all the contributing authors who write selflessly for Devotable. Without you, this project wouldn't exist. May we continue to create things that help edify and uplift believers and show Jesus Christ to this world.

Foreword

Trials and difficult situations find us all sooner or later. As people of faith, we're not promised smooth sailing, but we are promised a safe landing on the other shore. When we do face difficult situations, how do we handle them? Do we use those situations to help strengthen our resolve or do we let them beat us down and shake our faith? That might depend on the trial at hand. Whatever the case, we can find strength in knowing we're not alone; we all experience tests of faith.

As Christians, these trials often form us and make us who we are. How we handle them can set us on the course for our future. This is why it is so important to have mountain moving faith. Jesus tells us in Matthew 17:20 that we can literally move mountains if we have enough faith.

> *"Because of your little faith," He told them. "For I assure you: If you have faith the size of a mustard seed, you will tell this mountain, 'Move from here to there,' and it will move. Nothing will be impossible for you." (Matthew 17:20)*

When was the last time you actually believed you could move a physical mountain by having enough faith? Regardless if you believe you can move a whole mountain, the simple fact remains, our faith is strengthened or shaken by these trials. That is why we must persevere through them. We can use them to deepen our faith in Jesus Christ and His unwavering love for us.

The following devotions are stories, examples, and encouragement for facing those trials head on. We can learn from the experiences of others, how they handled tests of faith, and how God used those circumstances to bless them. We can read their accounts and see how God showed Himself faithful and true. We can hear words of wisdom from other faithful followers and see how we're not alone in this journey.

I hope these devotions bless you and encourage you to persevere through whatever this world is throwing at you. Use these devotions to equip yourself with the armor of God and press on toward the mark of a faithful follower. **-Landen Melton**

Day 1
Remain Faithful

I have fought the good fight, I have finished the race, I have kept the faith. There is reserved for me in the future the crown of righteousness, which the Lord, the righteous Judge, will give me on that day, and not only to me, but to all those who have loved His appearing. (2 Timothy 4:7-9)

Do you like a good fight? Most people would prefer not to fight. We teach our children to settle their differences in other ways because we learned the hard way that when people fight, someone often gets hurt. When we fought as children, we knew there was a good possibility it could be us who got hurt, and it often *was* us that got hurt. We now see fighting as a sign of immaturity, as a negative way to resolve differences.

Yet, the Apostle Paul told Timothy that he had fought a good fight. Was Paul a fighter? Spiritually speaking, yes. Paul endured much for the sake of Christ. He was beaten, stoned, shipwrecked, went without, ridiculed, persecuted, run out of numerous towns, etc. In spite of all he lived through, Paul could stand tall and proclaim that he remained faithful to the Lord; he never compromised the Gospel or backed down from proclaiming it, even while in prison because of it.

Why did Paul do it? Why did he think it was worth all the suffering? He knew that for the faithful there awaits a heavenly prize, a crown of righteousness that Christ Himself will give when they meet face-to-face. Paul had a purpose for living; he knew that what was before him was worth whatever he had to go through in this life. His eyes were fixed on Jesus. He was determined that no matter what, he would not give up; he would persevere until the end.

PERSEVERANCE

Life is not easy. It is full of ups and downs, good and bad times. It rarely goes smoothly. There are always times of suffering, whether those times be physical, mental, emotional, or spiritual. No one who lives for long is immune from life's sufferings. The faith walk is especially tough. The world does not like the faithful. Satan rules the world and is our enemy. He is out to destroy the faith of the faithful. God never promised us an easy road to heaven, but He did promise to be with us to help us remain faithful each step we take.

Live in such a way that you can like Paul, say that you have fought a good fight, that you have run well the race of life, you have finished what you started when you came to Christ, that you have been faithful to the end. Don't let Satan get the upper hand; resist him daily. It's not an easy fight to win, but it is a very winnable fight when you live submissively and obediently to Christ.

You won't win if you do not finish. There may be many obstacles along the way, but you must finish what you started. There are no timeouts in the race. Keep plugging away, and you will get to the finish line and great will be your reward in heaven.

What Scripture helps you to press on when you get down, discouraged, and defeated? Why?

_____

_____

_____

You are vulnerable when you neglect to read your Bible, pray, worship the Lord, and serve Him. Which of these areas do you need to focus on?

_____

_____

_____

Prayer

Lord, we at times want to give up. At times it's so hard to live by faith and not by sight. It's hard to be looked down upon by the world because of our faith. It's hard to stay disciplined with our reading of Your Word, prayer, and serving You. Lord, it's hard to stay strong and resist Satan; we have to admit there are times when we don't want to. Lord, help us to persevere, to remain faithful until we get home. In Jesus' name, Amen.

Jim Hughes is an ordained and retired pastor who has served the Lord in the church for 45 years, mainly as a bi-vocational pastor. He is also the author of nearly 50 books on faith and marriage. He has written a series of devotionals that cover every book of the Bible and a series of 6 books called *Marriage Quips.*

Connect with Jim at www.cthroughmarriage.weebly.com

Day 2
He Is Still the God of Bethel

Look, I am with you and will watch over you wherever you go. I will bring you back to this land, for I will not leave you until I have done what I have promised you. When Jacob awoke from his sleep, he said, "Surely the Lord is in this place, and I did not know it." He was afraid and said, "What an awesome place this is! This is none other than the house of God. This is the gate of heaven." Early in the morning Jacob took the stone that was near his head and set it up as a marker. He poured oil on top of it and named the place Bethel, though previously the city was named Luz. (Genesis 28:15-19)

I am the God of Bethel, where you poured oil on the stone marker and made a solemn vow to Me. Get up, leave this land, and return to your native land. (Genesis 31:13)

I can still remember the wave of sadness hitting me as we pulled out of the drive. My family and friends were waving to us in the rearview mirror, my new husband by my side. As we left the church and drove to our new home five hours away, tears of joy and sadness streamed down my face.

I was excited to begin a new life in a new town with the man I loved. But now that the excitement of the wedding was over, I faced the reality of leaving behind the familiar and entering a season of uncertainty.

Starting over in a new town proved difficult, and I spent much of that first year feeling discouraged, lonely, and unseen. Clinging to His Word, I soon found comfort buried within the story of Jacob. As I read about Jacob's time of transition and fear, I was reminded of who God is and what He has promised me.

Jacob was the son of Isaac and the twin brother of Esau, who infamously sold his birthright to Jacob for a bowl of stew. Once Esau realized what he had done, he threatened Jacob's life, forcing him to flee. Terrified, Jacob journeyed to Haran to work for his Uncle Laban.

The first night into his journey, Jacob dreamed of a ladder stretching from heaven to earth. Standing at the top of the ladder, God made him a promise, "Look, I am with you and will watch over you wherever you go. I will bring you back to this land, for I will not leave you until I have done what I have promised you" (Gen 28:15).

In the midst of Jacob's fear and insecurity, God reassured him that he was not alone. Jacob was so moved by this dream that he named the place Bethel, meaning, "The House of God."

During his time in Haran, Jacob worked for Laban, married two of his daughters, and had eleven sons. God blessed Jacob in his exile; so much so, that Jacob's father-in-law began to resent Jacob's success. It soon became clear that Jacob was no longer welcome in Laban's home. The Lord was once again moving in Jacob's life - enabling discomfort and rising tensions loosened his grip on his comfortable life.

For a second time, God spoke to Jacob in a dream. This time He told him to return home. It had been twenty years, and yet the command to return to his father's land and face Esau must have seemed like a death sentence. How could he possibly return?
But God calmed Jacob's heart with a simple reminder: "I am the God of Bethel" (Gen 31:13). In an instant, Jacob was reminded of the night he left home, when God saw him and comforted him. He was reminded of God's promise to be with him and to bring him home safely. It was all he needed to hear.

It was all I needed to hear, too.

What do you need to hear from God today? If you are walking down an unfamiliar road, wrestling with fear and doubt, I pray you would claim God's promise to Jacob as your own, for He is still the

God of Bethel. No matter where you are on your journey, He sees you. He is with you, guiding you. And He will be with you wherever you go.

Do you have a Bethel? A time when you clearly heard God's reassurance over your life? If you haven't already, write that promise down as a reminder of His love.

_____

_____

_____

Is God using difficult circumstances to loosen your grip on the life you want in order to give you the life He has planned? Confess your fears to Him today and ask Him to help release your control and yield to His.

_____

_____

_____

Prayer ╱

Father God, we thank You that You are El Roi - the God who sees. Our hearts sing knowing we are under Your watchful eye and Your protective wing. We confess our fears to You and ask for Your presence and provision. Be near to us, oh God. Amen.

_____

Mary Kathryn Tiller lives in East Texas with her husband, two children, and 30 head of cattle. Her passion is writing words that help others see Jesus more clearly.

Connect with Mary Kathryn at www.MaryKathrynTiller.com

Day 3
God Never Wastes a Thing

God is known in Judah; His name is great in Israel. His tent is in Salem, His dwelling place in Zion. There He shatters the bow's flaming arrows, the shield, the sword, and the weapons of war. Selah (Psalm 76:1-3)

I love a good bonfire, don't you? Usually the fire's set when everyone is winding down. The sun sets; we draw near to the warmth on a chilly evening and draw nearer to those we love. There may be dancing or better yet, storytelling. Laughter rings through the night mixed with tears and the smoky aroma of friendship is left lingering. The fire it breaks down barriers offering a sacred moment where heaven and earth collide. Deep healing happens in the fire.

Bonfires were born on the battlefield. After a long, hard-fought battle the wounded and weary gathered around to celebrate the victories of the day.

Yet, while most are celebrating, some may not see the victory. They see only loss, feel intense pain, and know the battle will rage on at daybreak. Yes, when the enemy can once again see, at first light, the fighting will begin anew. It's hard to muster up the will to fight again. Seeing the carnage strewn across the battlefield is just too much, and the questions come hard and fast.

Can you relate? Are you battle-weary from your most recent war?

Friend, whatever you see when you look out over the battleground isn't what God sees. Be encouraged. When you come asking, "What is it all for anyway?" God answers, "I have a

7

plan." He sees with heavenly perspective. Yes, He sees every hurt, every scar, every battle wound. He knows your pain and loss, but He also sees the purpose and ensures the victory.

Interestingly, another version of this passage says this is where God 'uses the broken arrows as kindling for His mighty bonfire' (TPT). Thankfully, while we're thinking nothing's been gained, God knows better. **God never wastes a thing**. I want to encourage you to stay in the fight. Persevere through your pain knowing whatever's been used against you God will turn to good.

Please, I beg you to take another look at your battlefield.

Imagine God's mighty hand sweeping across your war-torn wasteland. Scooping up every weapon used against you, He forms a massive pile. Then, before you can even ask what He's up to, He sets it all ablaze. The fire is enormous. The smoke rises and the sweet smell of sacrifice fills the air. He turns and motions for you to draw near His mighty bonfire. It's safe now. God is there. Won't you come and sit for a moment?

As you join God by the fire, He wraps His arm around you. Wiping away the tears, He leaves some smudges across your face. He doesn't explain it all, but promises one day you'll understand He never wastes a thing. **God takes every weapon that once wounded and sets our heart ablaze.** He takes the very things used against us and works them out to demonstrate His glory in us so others might be drawn to the flame.

Amazingly, that's what happens when the transforming power of the Holy Spirit breathes into our hearts. The Spirit burns up what's not of God leaving only what's pleasing to Him. Our wounds are healed resulting in a passionate love and fiery devotion to our Lord Jesus. God uses the purifying power of the Holy Spirit's fire to set a bonfire in our hearts igniting a flame that burns for all to see. We may come away with a little ash on our faces, but oh so beautiful for the work He's done in our lives. We walk away smelling like we've been with Jesus. It's the heavenly aroma of sacrifice burning on the battlefield.

What hurts, fears, losses, or wounds can you see God setting ablaze in His mighty bonfire?

_____

_____

_____

Write down ways you use the promise that God never wastes a thing to help you persevere through your pain and keep fighting your battle today.

_____

_____

_____

Prayer

Father God, You are such a good Father. You never take Your eyes off of me. You see my hard-fought battles. You catch every tear in a bottle. Thank You for taking what the enemy meant to destroy me and turning it into something good. Help me remember Your promise as I persevere through the pain. Remind me of Your goodness and set my heart ablaze for You.

_____

Amy Elaine Martinez is a wife, mom of two boys, an author, and inspirational speaker. She's also the host of Real Victory Radio who loves to share how she became a broken girl made whole through the transforming power of the Holy Spirit. Amy Elaine resides part-time in the historic towns of Guthrie, OK, and Castle Rock, CO. You'll usually find her at the local coffee shop writing or ministering across the table to a friend.

Connect with Amy at https://www.amyelaine.com

Day 4
Believing for Better

For our momentary light affliction is producing for us an absolutely incomparable eternal weight of glory. So we do not focus on what is seen, but on what is unseen. For what is seen is temporary, but what is unseen is eternal. (2 Corinthians 4:17-18)

When we read the phrase "momentary light affliction" found in 2 Corinthians 4:17 we might think it is dismissing our present problems as petty. Instead, it is meant to encourage us to realize they will seem that way in comparison to what God has in store for us.

Ever since I was young, I firmly believed God hears and answers every prayer. As I have grown older, I've learned more specifically that we can depend on Him to respond in one of three ways. He will say "Yes," "Not yet," or "No." In my life, there have been times that praying and receiving the third response has caused sorrow, and I have spent time wallowing in self-pity as I wondered why God seemingly failed me. Slowly, I am learning that His intent is not to disappoint His children with subpar substitutes for that which we pray. His goal has always been and will always be to answer our prayers with something better.

We often have a different definition of the word "better" than God does, however. Even when we put forth a determined effort to live in a selfless manner, our life perspective can still be self-centered as we only see how situations impact us now. We look at the word "better" through a small-picture, short-term lens, but He looks at it through a big-picture, infinity-long lens. He answers prayers according to what brings glory to Him and His kingdom. It may be difficult to see it through our human eyes, but His definition is always right, and it is always better than our definition.

In the midst of hardships such as financial loss, chronic illness, or the death of someone signifi-cant in our life, people often offer consolation in an attempt to assure us that God's plan will turn out to be better than we expected, and they offer the cliché, "There is a reason for everything."

When we are struggling to figure out the reason why God's answer is "No", that is the time to persevere in prayer as we recall His purpose in the past, His provision in the present, and His promises for the future. When we feel as if we have lost something, our loving God always provides us with a reason to believe for better. Friends, God has something better in store for us.

What are some past prayers of yours that God answered with "No" that turned out to be bless-ings?

_____

_____

_____

What are some tangible ways to remind yourself to persevere in prayer when circumstances turn out differently than you had hoped?

_____

_____

_____

Prayer

Dear Lord, thank You for caring deeply about our lives; our hopes, our dreams, and our hurts. Help us to see beyond our disappointment and instead see Your pur-pose, provision, and promises. Help us to trust that You know better when You an-swer our prayers differently than we expect. Thank You for Your amazing love. Amen.

Gwen Thielges resides in North Dakota where she is an author/blogger, church worship leader, and Kindermusik educator. She and her husband, Darren, have been blessed above and beyond what they could have ever imagined with three sons, one daughter, two daughters-in-law, and one grandson. She enjoys photography, writing music, and being a loyal fan in the stands for the endeavors of her family.

Connect with Gwen at https://gwenthielges.com

Day 5
Striving to Know Him

Let us strive to know the Lord. His appearance is as sure as the dawn. He will come to us like the rain, like the spring showers that water the land. (Hosea 6:3)

If you drive through California's Central Valley you'll witness mile after mile of farmland erupting with grapes, almonds, peaches, and crops of all kinds. If you take time to stop at one of the myriad produce stands dotting the Valley, your senses will be greeted with vibrant colors, tangy aromas, delectable textures, and sweet juices that will likely dribble down your chin.

Due to its fertile soil, the Central Valley is one of the most productive agricultural regions in the world. And yet, as I realized recently during one of our long drives, it's the water, the irrigation provided through an extensive system of reservoirs and canals, that takes the potential of the soil and converts it into land that literally bursts forth with life.

Our hearts, under the care of the Master Gardener, can become that same kind of rich soil. Through circumstances, through His Word, through the nudging of His Spirit as we go through our days, He stirs our souls. He's been stirring mine.

Yet it occurred to me the other day, as we drove through the Valley, that with all the stirring God does, with all the promptings He provides, it's up to us to open our hearts to Him. It's ours to strive to know Him, to press on, to drink of Him. He's the One who can make us flourish.

Striving though or pressing on, is sometimes easier said than done. Granted, just as soil naturally absorbs water, our hearts were made to respond to Him. Yet even when He's at work within us, we can be resistant. It can be simpler to sit mindlessly in front of the screen at the end of a day than to take time to draw close to Jesus. It can be easier to allow our hearts to fret and fume than to bring our anxieties to Him. After all, there is an Enemy of our souls who would much prefer we keep our eyes off Jesus.

So how do we flesh this out, this striving, this pressing on? There are so many possibilities.

For one thing, we can ruminate on God's truths. In Episode 1 of his new podcast, "Things Above," James Bryan Smith recommends taking to heart through daily meditation the words "I'm one in whom Christ dwells and delights." Undoubtedly, as we open our hearts to this simple yet profound truth we'll experience an impetus to get to know Jesus more intimately. We'll want to hold onto His "great and precious promises" that allow us to "share in His divine nature" (II Peter 1:4).

Another idea comes from Ruth Haley Barton, who in her book, *Sacred Rhythms*, suggests putting ourselves in the place of the blind beggar and telling Jesus what it is that we desire He do in our lives. Personally, this centering practice has brought me back time and again to my prayer that Jesus will draw me daily into His tender embrace.

Then there's the Psalmist, who encourages us to pour out our hearts to God in full assurance that He is our refuge (Psalm 62:8). Our lives hold all kinds of events that can range from the mildly disturbing to the hugely distressing, and what better response is there than to let out our frustrations or heartbreak to God? As He responds to our prayers we'll gain a deeper understanding of His character.

There are endless ways to acknowledge Him. We just have to start where we are and move toward Him.

How is God nudging and prompting you in the depths of your heart?

_____

_____

What regular practice could help you strive to know Him more intimately?

_____

_____

_____

Prayer

Lord God, Gardener of my soul, thank You for stirring the soil of my heart. I don't want these nudges and promptings to be for naught. My soul is crying out that now is the time to respond, now is the time to seek You in a fresh, more intimate way. Help my soul to drink in the depths of Your grace and goodness. As your Spirit works in me, cause me to be fruitful for You, that Jesus might be seen in me. Amen.

Tammy Gonzalez is a teacher, blogger, and recent empty-nester living in Los Angeles with her husband. She's currently learning about water's transformative effects even on the drought-tolerant plants under her care.

Connect with Tammy at https://tammygonzalez.org

Day 6
The Perspective That Helps Me Persevere

I keep the Lord in mind always. Because He is at my right hand, I will not be shaken. (Psalm 16:8)

There is no easy way to learn perseverance. It is learned the hard way - through pain, time, and practice. We cannot live in such a way that the need of perseverance is circumvented. As a recovering perfectionist, I used to try to live "perfectly" so that problems were prevented or solved ASAP.

This was my first valuable lesson on perseverance ironically. My "perspective" in regard to what pained me was totally wrong - unbiblical and unlike Jesus in every way. I somehow believed that if I lived a certain way, suffering could be optional.

As can be expected, this perspective did not serve me well. It exhausted me, leaving me completely frustrated. No matter how hard I tried, problems still confronted me and my family. A trouble-free existence did not seem plausible, even to a perfectionist.

This conflict with my perspective and my uncooperative reality came to light as I sat on my yellow couch lamenting to the Lord. He quickly brought to mind how contrary my perspective was compared to the Bible. Jesus not only experienced loads of suffering (and if anyone was "perfect" it was Him), He also clearly stated a perspective contrary to mine.

"I have told you these things so that in Me you may have peace. **You will have suffering**

in this world. Be courageous! I have conquered the world" (John 16:33).

I began to learn that the greater issue wasn't that I had suffering I didn't want or deserve at times. Rather, it was my perspective that was so unlike God's. Because my expectations were unrealistic, it hindered my ability to persevere. I learned that people who are frustrated the most are less likely to endure compared to those who are at peace with their circumstances.

That lesson from the Lord was a turning point for me in my life and in my faith. It helped me understand how different my perspective can be from God's. Since then, I have begun to implement a practice I learned from David to help offset this tendency of mine.

By keeping the Lord in mind, I am able to automatically consider, as well as inquire, what His perspective is on any given matter concerning me. The difference has had a profound impact because having the right expectations can make all the difference in my ability to persevere through what is painful.

Seeking God's viewpoint can totally change my feelings about my current circumstances. What I process as problematic or painful isn't always rooted in truth. What once was considered a challenge that needed solving can end up being a perspective that needs changing. Oftentimes, my "problems" have been as simple as that to remedy.

Suffering may not be optional, but it can sure be processed in such a way so that it isn't as overwhelming as I make it out to be. By remaining mindful of the Lord and drawing upon His perspective and grace, I am able to persevere through more than I ever thought possible. Like David, I am not shaken because God is at my right hand!

What is challenging you the most in your current season of life?

_____

_____

_____

How might God want to use this challenge in order to change your perspective regarding it?

_____

_____

_____

Prayer

Dear Lord, Give me eyes to see and perceive as You would, give me ears that process rightly, and give me a heart and mind that understands Your truth. Grant me Your perspective on my circumstances and teach me what You would have me to learn from this challenge. Use it for Your glory and my good.

_____

Gretchen Fleming is a Bible teacher who loves to encourage others in their faith. She is a national speaker and writer devoted to sharing God's Word so that lives are changed to the glory of God. She follows hard after Jesus because she knows God is our greatest reward.

Connect with Gretchen at https://gretchenfleming.com

Day 7
The Best Help in the Struggle

Stop your fighting—and know that I am God, exalted among the nations, exalted on the earth. (Psalm 46:10)

Are you in the middle of a battle? One you won't be able to win overnight? Do you know the best help to solve this struggle?

Are you a Fighter? Do you passively sit on the sidelines while a battle is ensuing? Or rise up determined never to give in? Maybe you are like me. You jump in with both feet and fight like a mighty warrior.

But what happens when the road is long, dusty, and you can no longer see the end? We can grow weary and discover our fighting plan works only for short-term battles.

The strength we had prided ourselves on begins to wane, and we become exhausted from the fight. The old method of "Pull up your bootstraps and keep moving" begins to fail.

I found myself in a place like this last month. My intentions were good and even honorable. I had set out determined to be God's warrior, fighting to the bitter end. After all, God created me strong.

Then slowly, but inevitably I grew tired. The fight for survival grew long and hard. My plan wasn't working. Have you ever been there?
Then in the middle of my persevering, God gave me a verse.

"Stop your fighting—and know that I am God, exalted among the nations, exalted on the earth" (Psalm 46:10).

At first, it seemed absurd. Why would God want me to cease striving in the middle of a battle? It seemed counterproductive.

However, as I explored what it means to be still, I learned that sitting with God is where one should start.

The original Hebrew word for being still is "Raphah" which carries with it a deeper meaning. To "be still" means so much more than what I had personally thought. As I read the definition, words and phrases jumped off the computer leaving me with all sorts of convictions - *stop striving, let go, willingly submit yourself to God and His control, surrender, leave alone, become weak, relax, be quiet, silent, inactive or still.*

Wow! It was evident I had been doing things in my strength, not God's. I was missing the Best Help.

As I began to practice sitting quietly before God, amazingly, my ability to endure increased tenfold.

When we become small, our Lord becomes BIG!
Letting go allows GOD to be GOD.
In the stillness, we will hear God's whispers.
We are never alone!

Unfortunately, all of us will struggle in life at some point. That is guaranteed. But what we decide to do is the key to surviving and enduring the journey well. Why not choose the best help in the struggle and be still with God.

When was the last time you stopped to be still with God?

_____

What are the things you need to let go of today so God can be in charge?

Prayer

Lord, sitting still is hard for me. Please forgive me when I jump too soon and start to fight. Thank You for your patience as You quietly wait for me to listen for Your voice. Teach me, Lord, to sit at Your feet. I know that You are God and I am not. Most of all thank You for never leaving me alone. I love You, Amen.

Maree Dee is a writer and speaker, passionate about embracing life in the midst of the unexpected. She is a work in progress, accepting God's grace and mercy every day. Maree believes together with God we can find incredible blessings along the way, even in the midst of the unexpected.

Connect with Mary Dee at www.embracingtheunexpected.com

Day 8
A Lesson in Failure

For you need endurance, so that after you have done God's will, you may receive what was promised. (Hebrews 10:36)

The word perseverance is defined as "steady persistence in a course of action, a purpose, a state, especially in spite of difficulties, obstacles, or discouragement." Perseverance is a choice. Each day, we make a decision to move forward.

A few years ago, I had to take a state exam. I will be the first to admit that I am not a great test taker. I usually get test anxiety and forget everything. And just as I had in previous years, I got into the testing room and forgot everything I studied. I failed the test. I was heartbroken, as I had to pass the test that year in order to get my teacher's certification.

I knew when I left the room that I had failed. I told my husband. He comforted me, suggesting that next time I pray about my test, continue to study, and figure out a way to keep myself calm during the test.

For a month, I studied and waited to register for the test again, and that test date came fast. This time, I decided not to stress; I created a studying system. I studied every day for three months, only breaking on the weekends. I prayed to calm my nerves before and after I studied.

On my test day, I walked into the room at ease and took the test. After seven days, my results came and I passed! Now, I could have given up, but I am not a person who gives up easily. I knew God allowed me to fail the test because I hadn't trusted in Him as I was studying. My decision to create a prayer circle around my test is what I believe made the difference.

I persevered in studying for this exam despite my dyslexia. I offered my disability to God, asked Him to help me overcome this challenge, and He answered my prayer. I share this to help other people realize that with God's help all things are possible. With God's help, I have overcome many of life's challenges, and there is nothing I can't overcome with His help.

Is there an area of your life where you have failed multiple times?

_____

_____

_____

Have you had some failures that taught you a lesson?

_____

_____

_____

Prayer

Father, thank You for giving us failures to teach us lessons. Forgive me for my lack of faith. Give me the strength to push through my doubts and build up my faith. Thank You for Your patience. Your humble child.

Paula Sanders Blackwell is a writer, educator, and entrepreneur. Paula is a self-proclaimed serial entrepreneur. In her short lifetime, she has owned a children's bookstore, and helped launch several nonprofit organizations. She is a life strategist who helps women recraft their lives. Paula is a woman passionate about faith and prayer.

Connect with Paula at http://paulablackwell.com

23

Day 9
One Battle. One Stone.
God Wins.

David said to the Philistine: "You come against me with a dagger, spear, and sword, but I come against you in the name of Yahweh of Hosts, the God of Israel's armies—you have defied Him." (1 Samuel 17:45)

Goliath! He's a mean, lean killing machine; ready to destroy anyone or anything in his path. He's almost 10-feet tall. He's wearing a bronze helmet. His coat of armor weighs as much as a 15-year-old boy. He has protected his muscular legs with bronze armor, and resting on his shoulder is a bronze spear whose tip weighs more than most bowling balls. If that's not enough, he has a personal armor bearer walking ahead of him carrying his shield. I told you he was mean. Oh, but he has one huge problem: he's on the wrong side of the law. He and his Philistine buddies have become emboldened in sin and defy the armies of the Most High God (Blessed be His Name).

Every day we wake up there are formidable opponents of our sanity, comfort, and peace defying our faith and our God. If we allow them to back us into a corner and taunt us every time their discouraging voices ring out, our faith wavers and we fear the worst. Bills, sickness, relationship problems, the endless bad news cycles, guilt feelings, and doubt all array themselves like the Philistine army who struck fear in the hearts of God's people, and one very mean giant leads the charge. That giant is our will; that deep essence within us that drives action. I mean that force that decides whether you will persevere under pressure or give up. I mean that tenacity to move forward with the measure of faith God gives to all people; that if we surrender it to Him, it will grow strong enough to move giants and even mountains.

The Israelite army had somehow forgotten the many times God had defeated their enemies in the past. They lost sight of the victories He won when they willed to keep faith in Him. They allowed the Philistine forces to redouble their efforts, enlist the services of the foul-mouthed giant from Gath, and he continually taunted God's people, striking layers of fear into their hearts and into the heart of their king who lacked the spiritual courage to answer his attacks.

Enter David, the shepherd boy. You see, David was a young man who trusted God to overcome all obstacles in his life. He remembered the many times God came through for him in seemingly impossible situations. So, when he heard the vulgar giant blaspheming God's name, he did not cower. No! David, with the faith to move forward against all odds, allowed God to fight his battles. He cooperated with God and chose five smooth stones to meet the giant in one of the fiercest battles ever—the spiritual warfare of the will. He willed to believe God during the times of greatest trials. And with one smooth stone hurled from David's sanctified sling, the giant was defeated.

What do you do when the giants of life come your way? May I suggest something to you? Throw stones at them! Okay, throw the Stone at them. Jesus Christ is the Chief Cornerstone. He is the Rock upon which He built His church. He is the spiritual Rock who quenched Israel's thirst in the wilderness. When you encounter giants, who taunt and attempt to discourage you, let Jesus defeat them. Never give up. Never give in. Never allow any opponent, no matter how formidable, to cause to you lose sight of Jesus Christ, the answer to every problem you will ever encounter. If the Great Stone of our faith has a 100% victory rate, I think it's safe to put all our trust in Him; how about you?

How can your example, like David's, inspire others to move forward in faith through any obstacle?

_____

_____

_____

How many times has Jesus defeated your giants of doubt and fear in the last 30 days? Write down just two. It will encourage you the next time you are challenged to trust God.

_____

_____

_____

Prayer

Lord, please teach us to trust You in every situation, no matter how dire. In the name of Jesus we pray, Amen.

_____

L. David Harris is an author of scores of books and well over 1,000 articles, publisher, public speaker, and social media evangelist who loves God more than life itself.

Connect with L. David Harris at www.LDavidHarris.com

Day 10
Keep Running!

...Let us run with endurance the race that lies before us, keeping our eyes on Jesus, the source and perfecter of our faith, who for the joy that lay before him endured a cross and despised the shame and has sat down at the right hand of God's throne. (Hebrews 12:1-2)

British track athlete Derek Redmond won many races during his career, but is perhaps best known for his "failed" 400 meter run in the 1992 Olympic Games in Barcelona, Spain. Midway through the semi-final race, Redmond tore his hamstring muscle. Collapsing to the track, Redmond knew his dream of winning an Olympic gold medal was over. Despite the physical and emotional pain, however, the injured Redmond got to his feet and began to hobble toward the finish line. Before long, Redmond was joined by his father, Jim, who came down from the stands to assist his son in covering the remaining distance. Although he was disqualified from the event, Redmond, held by his father, crossed the finish line to a standing ovation from fans.

As followers of Jesus, we, too, participate in a race. Ours, however, is not one of physical prowess, but of spiritual endurance. Our pace is often slowed by the opponents of fear and disbelief, and our sin threatens to bring us to a crippling stop. Still, we strive to finish. There are no participation trophies in the race of life. We must keep running!

The truth is that we do not run alone. Jesus goes before us and stands with us. The author of Hebrews states that Jesus was "...tested in every way as we are, yet without sin" (Hebrews 4:15). Jesus has already run the race of life, and he completed it to perfection. Jesus is "...the source and perfecter of our faith..." (Hebrews 12:2). He is "...the Alpha and the Omega, the First and the Last, the Beginning and the End" (Revelation 22:13). Jesus is with us as we crouch at the starting blocks and as we cross the finish line. He is alongside us every step of the way, challenging and encouraging us to keep going. Even when we stumble and fall, Jesus races to our aid to assist us in finishing.

If you personally are tired and weary of running a race that seems more like a marathon than a sprint, I'd like to encourage you to simply take the next step. If shame is slowing your pace, know that Jesus has already carried all of your sin to the cross. If you have faltered, failed, floundered, or fallen down, Jesus is ready to carry you to the end. Keep running! Finish the race! The prize is worth the persevering.

What things tend to slow your pace in life's race (i.e., sin, worry, doubt)?

_____

_____

_____

Have you asked Jesus to run life's race with you, to even carry you to its finish? If not, why not now?

_____

_____

_____

Prayer

Dear Jesus, help me as I continue to run life's race. Remind me of Your presence. Encourage and sustain me. Thank You for dying on a cross so that I can live with You forever. In Your holy name I pray, Amen.

Chuck Kralik is a pastor and author. He enjoys spending time with his family and friends and cheering for his favorite teams, the Nebraska Cornhuskers and Chicago Cubs.

Connect with Chuck at http://www.chuckkralikauthor.com

Day 11
Persevering in Prayer

He then told them a parable on the need for them to pray always and not become discouraged: "There was a judge in a certain town who didn't fear God or respect man. And a widow in that town kept coming to him, saying, 'Give me justice against my adversary.' For a while he was unwilling, but later he said to himself, 'Even though I don't fear God or respect man, yet because this widow keeps pestering me, I will give her justice, so she doesn't wear me out by her persistent coming.'" Then the Lord said, "Listen to what the unjust judge says. Will not God grant justice to His elect who cry out to Him day and night? Will He delay to help them? I tell you that He will swiftly grant them justice. Nevertheless, when the Son of Man comes, will He find that faith on earth?" (Luke 18:1-8)

How often do you give up when the going gets tough?

I've given up on sports in which I never excelled due to a lack of coordination. I've given up on New Year's resolutions, exercise programs, and other healthy habits. I'm sure you have done the same.

But I have given up most often on one important thing, and that is prayer.

Why?

Persevering in prayer is hard. Just like sticking to good habits that don't show instant results (hello pushups and planks), prayer doesn't always give you what you want, when you want it.

If you've prayed for a dream to come true, a path to be revealed, or a lost soul to turn to God, yet still have no answer, you may feel discouraged. I know I have.

Discouragement can prevent us from persevering in prayer. It's Satan's way of putting distance between us and God. It causes us to doubt if God keeps His promises or if He even hears us pray at all.

Yet Jesus wants us to persevere in prayer. In Luke 18:1 He tells us "to pray always and not become discouraged." He knows that discouragement can be a roadblock to persevering in prayer. That's why He painted a word picture of what persistent prayer looks like.

In Jesus' parable, a widow continuously approached a harsh, worldly judge asking for justice. Because the widow kept pestering the judge, she wore down his resolve and he granted her request.

Of course, our loving Heavenly Father is no unrighteous judge. But as a sinful earthly father knows to provide good gifts to his children (Matt. 7:9-11), our perfect heavenly Father is eager to give us good things if we keep asking for them.

In Luke 18:7 Jesus indicates that God wants to grant justice to His followers and will not delay in helping them. We must be faithful in prayer like the persistent widow to show God we are seeking His help.

Persistent prayer is a mystery. We don't know when God will answer; timing is the Father's business. Yet for some reason, the Lord God Almighty wants to hear us ask, sometimes again and again, for our prayers to be answered.

Maybe persistent prayer is more about changing us to be more like Jesus than about receiving the answer. Perhaps persevering in prayer shapes our spiritual lives much more than if we got what we wanted, when we wanted it.

I love hearing stories of people who prayed for years and finally received their answers. Their stories encourage me to persist in prayer, because I don't know when my answer will come. They didn't know either at year five, fifteen, or fifty.

Even if I never receive the answer I want, my faith grows every time I pray. My relationship with God deepens and peace rests on my heart with each request. Perfect peace can only be found in God's presence.

I've learned that discouragement is no longer a roadblock. It's a trigger to pray more frequently, fervently, and faithfully than before. Satan tries to use it to trick me into giving up. But Jesus transforms my discouragement into yet another reason to pray.

He will do the same for you as you persevere in prayer.

What particular prayer have you given up on due to discouragement?

_____

_____

_____

How can persistent prayer make you more like Jesus, especially if you don't receive an answer right away?

_____

_____

_____

Prayer

Heavenly Father, thank You for valuing my prayers. When I feel discouraged in prayer that has not been answered, prompt me to keep praying and draw me closer to You. I trust You to answer all my prayers in Your perfect timing. In Jesus' name, Amen.

Sarah Geringer is an author, blogger, and artist who writes about finding peace in God's Word.

She lives in Missouri with her husband and three children, right in the heart of prime viewing area for the Great Solar Eclipses of 2017 and 2024. When not reading or writing, Sarah enjoys nature walks, gardening, and baking. She's always up for good conversations with friends.

Connect with Sarah at https://www.sarahgeringer.com/

Day 12
Persevering Through Temptations

A man who endures trials is blessed, because when he passes the test he will receive the crown of life that God has promised to those who love Him. (James 1:12)

Do you struggle with temptations? I do. Trials are temptations and sometimes strike without warning.

Satan's greatest weapon is a temptation. Adam and Eve fell victim to its cunning. Cain caved in to its evil intention. Peter couldn't stop himself from denying Christ, and Paul's persecution of Christians captures the damage it causes to God.

I think you'll agree with me when I say it takes perseverance in overcoming temptation. In fact, without reliance on Christ the spiritual strength necessary to withstand them stay elusive.

James' message is powerful and shows God's grace, faithfulness, and loyalty. And it's in persevering through temptation we discover this awesome truth.

Those who receive salvation gain spiritual courage to endure the devil's temptation. This power comes from Christ.

When Christ prevailed over the devil's temptations (Matthew 4:1-11) it showed His power over darkness. Jesus used perseverance to defeat Satan's attempts by showing him God's truth. In our society, we see a life without Christ loses the battle with temptation. But as a believer in Jesus, God gives us the strength to crush temptation.

God's approval comes from His grace through faith and accepting Christ as the way to heaven. It's Christ who is God's crown. We know this truth because Christ anoints us with the Holy Spirit. The Holy Spirit is God's way of allowing us to experience His presence. The Holy Spirit leaves no doubt to God's existence.

Now that God gave us the Holy Trinity, it fulfils His promise. The best part is the love God has for those who pick up their crosses and walk in His Spirit. In return, we discover our love to fulfill His purpose.

When I'm tempted I have a choice. I can rely on Christ or give in to sin. When I fail and allow it to take over, troubles emerge. This freedom of choice is significant because God is watching.

The interesting part of giving in to temptation is that Christ supplies a way to amend the wrong. It's called repentance. Until I repent, my life stays unmanageable. I become distant from His presence and a spiritual void enters my soul. But when I humble myself before Christ without reservation then I discover God's forgiveness. As a result of repentance, my reunion with God returns and my spirit is renewed.

As shown above, persevering through temptations is possible and brings positive results. Remember everyone faces temptations (1 Corinthians 10:13). The point is, with Christ they lose power, and we draw closer to God.

What do you do when temptation leads to sin? Write down a time when temptation led to sin.

_____

_____

_____

Are you willing to repent? Do so by asking God for forgiveness.

_____

_____

_____

Prayer

God, here I am. Do with me as You want. I ask You for the strength to persevere through temptation. How can I better serve You and others? I ask this in You Christ, Amen.

_____

Walter Kahler is a believer in Christ the Son of God who loves writing on the way God works in his life. He enjoys sharing his experiences with Christ and the impact it continues to have on his life. He's grateful for the gift of Salvation and how he applies Christ's truth to everyday problems.

Connect with Walter at https://achristianmindset.org/

Day 13
Life Gets Wild: Stop Trying To Tame the Spirit

Then Jesus returned from the Jordan, full of the Holy Spirit, and was led by the Spirit in the wilderness. (Luke 4:1)

This year I've had a couple projects that have taken me to locations like Africa and Australia. Part of what I enjoy besides working in these amazing places is learning about or becoming aware of the different types of animals and insects that are native to these regions.

My awareness, and more importantly, my behavior, shifts due to my new surroundings. Whether I'm checking my shoes for spiders, avoiding a particular bird, or not walking in some areas with food, I become more prepared to deal with possible wildlife interactions. If not, then I fail to respect the nature of whatever I cross paths with, and often that's how we later read headlines or hear reports of individuals falling victim to what they encounter.

In order to persevere in the wilderness, you adapt to it. That doesn't mean you must become like it, but it does mean your thoughts and actions have observed things and now you must deal with the new situation appropriately. Just as a child growing up in a gang neighborhood navigates the social dynamic there or a woman charged with leading a male dominated office, both are keenly aware they have a mission in spite of the predators.

Christ was led into the wilderness by the Holy Spirit prior to being crucified. He faced trials for forty days. His environment had changed, and possibly hoping to catch Jesus in a compromising position, Satan threw every imaginable test and temptation at Him.

The Son of God adjusted during that trying time, never taking for granted that in the wild, respecting danger meant not tempering nor trying to tame the fullness of the Holy Spirit.

Our lives are no different. It doesn't take much for us to feel out of sorts. Identity theft. Emergency surgery. Family situations. Things get wild, our imaginations get wilder and we still come with some very tame responses and prayers.

At our disposal exists the Holy Spirit, but we might be approaching the path of the wilderness and only partially tapping into it. Just as you wouldn't allot one hundred miles of fuel for a two hundred mile trip, our limiting capacity and expectations will leave us empty and stranded in the wilderness. With the Holy Spirit we can claim victory for the Kingdom.

Prepare for the season in the wilderness by asking the Holy Spirit to pour into you fully, stay hungry to serve the Lord, and allow Him to lead you through temptations, no matter how wild and outrageous.

Where are you not fully respecting the wilderness and missing your opportunity to persevere?

_____

_____

_____

How are you limiting the power of God to meet your human expectations?

_____

_____

_____

Prayer

Merciful Father, I'm rebuking any spirit of hesitation over my life. I believe that the Holy Spirit's power will cover me and my household. Destroy beliefs that are holding me back and begin to transform the way I pray, live, and think-wildly, in Your precious name, Amen!

Quentin G. Love is the son, grandson, and great-grandson of ministers. Quentin's success is rooted in providing a judgment free atmosphere to witness and have shared dialogue. He's a follower of Christ who is simply striving to walk in obedience and share the Word of God as instructed in Mark 16:15.

Connect with Quentin at www.quentinglove.com

Day 14
Perseverance in Waiting

When Joshua was near Jericho, he looked up and saw a man standing in front of him with a drawn sword in His hand. Joshua approached Him and asked, "Are You for us or for our enemies?" "Neither," He replied. "I have now come as commander of the Lord's army." Then Joshua bowed with his face to the ground in worship and asked Him, "What does my Lord want to say to His servant?" The commander of the Lord's army said to Joshua, "Remove the sandals from your feet, for the place where you are standing is holy." And Joshua did so. (Joshua 5:13-15)

One day I had to stop at the DMV with my four-year-old son. That was the day he learned the meaning of the word "patient." The next day at the fabric store, his patience in waiting for me was wearing pretty thin. He begged for me to let him get out of the cart. "I will be patient," was his promise. Another customer standing nearby burst out laughing. While the story may be funny, patience is no laughing matter.

Patience develops perseverance.

Patience is a virtue; one of which I am greatly lacking. If I see something that needs to be done, I do it. If I see a problem, I try to solve it. The problem with that is that I am working solely on my own and not depending on or even looking to God for answers.

Joshua is a great biblical figure to study to see how patience should be done. In the first few chapters of the book of Joshua, we read that he was promoted to lead Israel, taking over the position of Moses, to scope out the city of Jericho, and make plans to defeat it.

But...God had a plan of His own. First, He required that all of the fighting men of Israel get circumcised. That put off the attack for at least a few days. Then as Joshua approached Jericho, possibly to do a little more investigating or perhaps pray, he is stopped by an Angel, the Lord Himself. Joshua takes the time to stop and worship when told to take off his shoes; he was standing on holy ground. Instead of getting upset with the interruption, he was patient and did what needed to be done in that moment.

Unfortunately, my worship sometimes feels more like "can we hurry up and get this over with?" Or my devotions each day are something to cross off my to-do list. I am not being patient, and I'm not allowing God to speak to my heart. What about all the prayer requests we throw at God? We often make demands expecting God to answer according to our terms, usually that's immediately. However, God is not a genie, and He does not work in our time frame. He can see the bigger picture of our lives, He loves us, and wants what He knows is best for us. It is often in that waiting time God helps us to develop and grow spiritually. Patience in the waiting helps us build perseverance and dependence on God.

Each one of us needs to live and work on God's time-table. Sometimes things happen quickly while other things may take years to come to fruition. Wherever you find yourself today be patient, seek God's timing, and persevere. In your waiting ask God what He has for you. What does He want to teach you? Perhaps there are other factors that have not yet fallen into place to where He can answer your prayer. Whatever the case, persevere in your patience. Doing things on your own, outside of God's will never works out anyway.

Can you think of a time in your life where you had to wait on God? Maybe you had to wait for a job, a spouse, or healing.

_____

_____

_____

Write down some areas of your life where you know you need to be patient in waiting on God. Can you lift those areas up to Him today and allow Him to have total control of your life?

_____

_____

_____

Prayer

Dear Lord, waiting is so hard for me sometimes, but I know I need to wait on You. Give me perseverance to wait patiently and see where Your hand is at work in my life. Amen.

_____

Ruth O'Neil, born and raised in upstate New York, attended Houghton College. She has been a freelance writer for more than 20 years, publishing hundreds of articles in dozens of publications. Ruth spends her spare time quilting, scrapbooking, and camping with her family.

Connect with Ruth at http://ruthoneil.weebly.com/

Day 15
Effort + Faith = Grace?

For this very reason, make every effort to supplement your faith with goodness, goodness with knowledge, knowledge with self-control, self-control with endurance, endurance with godliness, godliness with brotherly affection, and brotherly affection with love. (2 Peter 1:5-7)

Since my early days as a young believer, I've understood the biblical doctrine of grace. Well, I understood it at a basic level. As I learned about the 5 Solas of Protestant Reformation theology, the importance of God's grace solidified even more for me.

One of the first Bible verses I memorized was—

For you are saved by grace through faith, and this is not from yourselves; it is God's gift (Ephesians 2:8).

And I discovered and noted many other Scriptures that confirmed the important theological truth of God's grace alone as the believer's confidence in the assurance of our salvation.

The popular expression "Jesus + nothing = everything" says it all. But one day I came across these verses:

For this very reason, make every effort to supplement your faith with goodness, goodness with knowledge, knowledge with self-control, self-control with endurance, endurance with godliness, godliness with brotherly affection, and brotherly affection with love (2 Peter 1:5-7).

Whoa...wait a minute! How can you add anything to faith? Isn't faith itself a gift of God's grace? Why would the Apostle Peter exhort believers to "...make every effort to add to your faith..."?

So, I checked the original Greek text, other Bible versions, and sought counsel from reliable commentaries. All my study revealed it meant exactly what it said.

Once again, I understood the importance of context. As I read the preceding two verses (2 Peter 1:3-4) and those immediately following (2 Peter 1:8-11), I realized it was one continuous thought, just as our redemption is one continuous process.

I saw how it spoke of what perseverance in faith is. What God began in us He will complete until the day we see Jesus face to face (Phil 1:6).

So, how can we "make every effort" and not become absorbed in our own efforts to gain God's redemption? Or, not get sucked into working for our salvation?

Faith is all about trust, a personal trust in the Lord, Himself (Hebrews 11:6). We need to live by faith and exercise our faith to remain spiritually healthy. Just as our physical bodies need healthy food and exercise, so also our faith needs to be fed and exercised.

This list of spiritual qualities describes how we can persevere in our faith. They speak of the working of God's Spirit living in us and transforming us, and are similar to what the Apostle Paul says are the Fruit of the Spirit (Galatians 5:22-23).

The context of these verses helps us understand how important these qualities are for us to persevere in our faith and reflect God's Spirit in us. Goodness implies integrity or moral excellence, the effect of God's goodness at work in us. The knowledge spoken of here is insight and understanding of the Lord Himself, a personal knowledge and understanding of who He is. Self-control results from continuing to submit our self-will to God, and endurance is like the persistence needed for running a marathon, to persevere to the finish line. Godliness speaks of an internal self-discipline through the power of God's Spirit.

Brotherly affection is simply a genuine care and concern for others and is linked to love; an un-selfish and unconditional love, the way God loves us.

Peter tells us these qualities need to increase in our life (2 Peter 1:8) as we continue to trust in God daily. This is the essence of spiritual growth and the key to persevering in faith, our life submitted to Him as the Holy Spirit is at work in us.

What do you see as your greatest hindrance to growing and persevering in your faith?

_____

_____

_____

Of the seven spiritual qualities Peter speaks of—goodness, knowledge, self-control, endurance, godliness, brotherly affection, love—which do you think is the one you most need to grow in? How can you do that?

_____

_____

_____

Prayer

Lord, help me to continue to grow spiritually and persevere as I trust in You daily. Encourage me to add these spiritual qualities in my life, as You produce the fruit of Your Spirit in me.

Trip Kimball is a teacher, writer, pastor, missionary, disciple-maker, mentor—I love Jesus, my wife, children, grandkids, and the beach!

Connect with Trip at https://www.word-strong.com/

Day 16
Faith for the Unthinkable

She placed the child in it and set it among the reeds by the bank of the Nile. (Exodus 2:3a)

With each new baby, my sleep was interrupted and schedules changed. Like other couples, my husband and I met new responsibilities and decisions. When a baby is born, everything changes.

One woman who knew change like no one else was Moses' mother, Jochebed. At the time of Moses' birth, the Hebrews were multiplying in record numbers. Pharaoh feared they would outnumber the Egyptians and rebel, so he "...commanded all his people: "You must throw every son born to the Hebrews into the Nile, but let every daughter live.'" (Exodus 1:22)

A new baby should bring joy, but Jochebed and her family were faced with unthinkable change. I wonder how many screams and sobs she heard as baby boys were snatched from mother's arms. Instead of delight, the unknown overshadowed every moment.

Jochebed was a Levite, a member of a priestly tribe. She knew the stories of faith and the character of God. She remembered God's promise to Abraham that the Hebrews would become as numerous as the stars. It was happening right before her eyes.

But knowing doesn't lessen the reality of trials and the pain we experience. Like any mom, Jochebed wanted to protect her son. Did she muffle his cries, so he wouldn't be heard? What do you do in dire situations when there appears to be no way out? Moses would grow. It would become obvious he should have been killed.

With the tenacity of a mother's love, Jochebed weaves a strong papyrus, waterproof basket and places her son in it. No, it isn't a basket because he has outgrown his first one. She places it in the crocodile infested Nile River, courageously releasing Moses to God's care.

In God's providence, an Egyptian princess found him and needed a nurse. Miriam, who was watching her brother's rescue from the river bank, got Jochebed. She cared for Moses until he was weaned. Once more, mother and son say goodbye. We never hear from Jochebed again except later in a New Testament reference (Hebrews 11:23).

We face challenges in many ways. I have met financial difficulties and unexpected widowhood. Perhaps you are experiencing family conflicts, health issues, or a difficult work environment. Jochebed shows us, even in the most trying times, we can choose to act in faith, not fear, and trust God. Sometimes, we need to let go of our dreams and desires and live the different plans God has for us. His blessings may come not in a resolution but in seeing Him work in our trial.

Jochebed's circumstances didn't change. Neither did her faith in God. In Hebrews 11:23, she is remembered, "By faith, after Moses was born, he was hidden by his parents for three months, because they saw that the child was beautiful, and they didn't fear the king's edict." Jochebed shows us how confronting challenges with faith brings rewards, some she never anticipated or lived to know about. That is trust and that is faith.

The stories of faith strengthened Jochebed. Where do you lean when you face challenges and disappointments? Do you have a life verse? If not, find Scriptures to encourage you.

_____

_____

_____

Jochebed was a resourceful woman. God prepared her with the talent of basket making. What gifts and resources has God given you as you responsibly persevere through difficulties?

_____

_____

_____

Prayer

Father, help me cling to Your character, that You are all-knowing, wise, and loving. Direct me to encouragement and wisdom from Your Word that I may act responsibly and with faith as I deal with life trials. May I bring glory to Your name. In Jesus' name, Amen.

Marilyn Nutter is a writer for print and online sites, a Bible teacher, and facilitator for a grief support group. Suddenly widowed in 2011, Lamentations 3:22-23 has sustained her in a new life chapter.

Connect with Marilyn at www.marilynnutter.com

Day 17
Delivered from My Enemies

"I called to the Lord, who is worthy of praise, and I was saved from my enemies."
(Psalm 18:3)

I remember some time, not that long ago, when doing simple, everyday things felt like climbing the steepest mountain or having to lift a heavy truck. Depression's darkness covered me, but I clung for dear life onto the hope that my God would make a way, and that it would not always be this hard. By the grace of God today is that day. I am free.

I know I am not alone. There is an evident soul crisis washing over our society and culture. Suicide rates are alarming, families are broken left and right. What the Bible predicted, that good would be called bad and bad would be called good, is right before our eyes. Peace feels ever fleeting, and heaven knows we need it right now.

Yet, even when the shadows of night seem overwhelming, it only takes the break of dawn to change absolutely everything. In Psalm 18, David worships God who delivered him from his enemies in a time of war. If a time of war is not what's at hand, I don't know what is. But David's worship is our personal and prophetic promise.

David said of God, "He reached down from heaven and took hold of me; He pulled me out of deep waters. He rescued me from my powerful enemy and from those who hated me, for they were too strong for me" (Psalm 18:16–17).

Whether we face difficulties of our own design or hardship that came undeserved, the Lord cares about our predicament. We don't have to be strong enough. It is often when we break that He can make us whole again. In our surrender and worship, God delivers us.

God can deliver us from all our enemies, even when this enemy is ourselves. The war that rages inside is the one we need to be delivered from the most. We try to figure it out, to be strong on our own, but we can't. God says, "Come to me, child. It's okay. I will give you peace and rest. I love you."

I know trusting God is sometimes easier said than done, but we don't need to trust Him for a specific outcome. We just need to trust Him. We need to choose to believe that He is good. We need to trust that He can give us the peace and strength we need to face the storm.

Often the untangling of our hearts and minds is all we really need to move forward and out of our troubles.

What situation in your life is so discouraging that when you think of it, you don't feel like worshipping the Lord?

_____

_____

_____

What would deliverance from this situation look like?

_____

_____

_____

Prayer

Father, I worship You. Like David, I will rejoice in the God of my salvation. You have delivered me before, and You will do it again. I choose to believe that You are good. You are faithful and just, O Lord. There is none like You. Light a new fire in my soul. Remove what is not of You and teach me to follow Your ways alone. In Jesus' name, I pray, Amen!

Just like you, **Caroline Bellemare** wants more of God. That's why she writes about real life and how to bring God's Kingdom into every aspect of it. She is married to her best friend, JB, and is the mother of Imela Christy. She loves travelling, books, and drinking Earl Grey tea.

Connect with Caroline at https://carolinebellemare.com

Day 18
The Formula to Forgiveness

You planned evil against me; God planned it for good to bring about the present result—the survival of many people. (Genesis 50:20)

I am convinced that one of the most difficult life tasks to push through is stale cereal. Laugh all you want, but the first time you bite in expecting the crunch of the Captain and you experience a chewy capsule of petrified sugar and refined grains, you'll have zero remaining doubts.

Possessing stale cereal probably speaks to a condition of abundance. You clearly had enough food in your cupboard to choose from, neglecting to choose the cereal for quite some time. Joseph found himself in a place of abundance. He and the Egyptians had so much food that they survived a seven-year famine and helped surrounding countries stay alive as well.

For those of you familiar with the story, you know the Egyptians received some divine influence about the coming famine. They stock-piled grains to prepare themselves.

The Egyptians and surrounding countries were thankful but had no idea of the full extent of God's plan. God's plan was bigger than feeding empty bellies and preserving lives. It was to display the most powerful act of love in the world... forgiveness.

God cares so much about forgiveness that He orchestrated His divine plan strategically placing Joseph in a position to not only be a provider for God's people but also show forgiveness to his brothers for their heinous acts years ago. God worked out something good from the ashes of evil.

Joseph's life shows us that forgiveness is a decision. He made the decision to forgive his brother's while he was in the pit where they dropped him years before. That's why when it came time to be reunited, he had no issues forgiving. He had spent the previous years processing his emotions and anger. He had to persevere through his emotions until they fell in line with God's will. Joseph had to choose forgiveness every day.

Most often individuals have no idea where the lines are drawn between forgiveness and unforgiveness. They feel as if they have decided in their minds to forgive, but their emotions indicate that's not true.

Your emotions often aren't the greatest indicator of your progress and pursuit of forgiveness. You too must make the decision every day to forgive. Your emotions will not follow immediately, but they will eventually catch up, as you have set your life on a trajectory towards healing, not embitterment.

Time heals, but it doesn't forgive. Only you can forgive. Soon you will make a habit of forgiving. That sounds like our Lord doesn't it? He is always quick to forgive.

I recommend this exercise: Wake up each morning and write the name of your offender. The first few times you will find this very difficult to push through. Just the sight of his/her name may evoke strong emotions. It will get easier and easier, and eventually, you will be able to write, say, and even smile at the mention of his/her name... just as the Lord does with us.

Whose name when mentioned elicits a strong emotion of anger in you? There may be underlying unforgiveness. Ask the Lord to reveal names to you and write them down.

_____

_____

_____

How do you feel about yourself and your past mistakes? Is your name the highest one on the list to forgive? If so, why do you think it's been difficult to forgive yourself?

_____

_____

_____

Prayer

Father, we ask You for strength and wisdom concerning our pursuit of perseverance and forgiveness. We want to learn by Your example in how You have forgiven us. Help us to see our offender as You see them, with grace and love. In Christ's name, Amen.

_____

Joshua Troester is the founding pastor of Live Church in Republic, MO. His primary goal is to bring people together to teach them God's Word in a practical and relatable way for everyday life. Josh and his wife Tara have one son Grayson, and are surrounded by a tremendous church and ministry community.

Connect with Josh at http://wearelive.church

Day 19
Waiting for God's Surprises

Wait for the Lord; be strong and courageous. Wait for the Lord. (Psalm 27:14)

I like to tell my daughter about things we'll be doing. Except sometimes I don't give her all the details. I tell her it's a surprise which builds eager anticipation. She loves surprises, because she knows I only promise her good things.

She'll often torture me trying to get more details, asking 20 more questions, even though she knows I ultimately will not give away the surprise. She'll also invariably always ask, "Is it time yet?" But when I tell her about the upcoming surprise, I give her a timeline. She's still learning the concept of time, so I'll have to explain to her that it's either after her big sleep or after her mid-afternoon nap. I just know that I better be ready for whichever time period I tell her.

I feel like God tells us that He has wonderful surprises in store for us. Except He doesn't provide the same time line I do to my daughter. He doesn't say, at 5:00 pm on October 16th, this particular thing will happen. What He says is, "Kaysi, I'll do such and such." And me being like my four year old, says, "Yes, God, but can we do this on my schedule?"

I'm learning that's not how it works.

Yesterday in church, there was a presentation on the Israelites moving from Egypt to the Promised Land. A trip that could have taken 11 days ultimately took 40 years. God used that time to build the characters and habits of those who would enter the Promised Land. There was a lot of grumbling along the way, but God doesn't go by the grumbling, He goes by when He knows we are ready for what He has in store.

Imagine, if I think I know how to give good gifts to my daughter? What more precious gifts God has in store for you and me? What are you trusting Him for? What are you waiting on Him for; to reveal His surprises? I'm also learning that He doesn't leave you without clues, just like I share with my daughter; you only need to look and listen for what they are.

How are you waiting on God for the good things He has in store for you?

_____

_____

_____

Do you tend to get frustrated and want to take matters in your own hands or do you lean on Him for His understanding?

_____

_____

_____

Prayer

Dear Heavenly Father, we thank You for our waiting time. Help us to use it wisely as You build us up and refine our characters. Help us to see this time for what it is: a chance to learn of the depth of Your love for us. Help us not to get disheartened as we wait for Your perfect timing.

Kaysian C. Gordon is a writer, speaker, and Bible teacher. After years of education in the financial arena, Kaysian recently felt the call to start writing a faith blog, which she shares on her website www. kaysigordon.com and on social media. She teaches her church's youth class and speaks to various women's groups. Kaysian has felt the call to share with others the lessons God has been teaching her.

Connect with Kaysian at www.kaysigordon.com

Day 20
Through Faith

Therefore, since we have been declared righteous by faith, we have peace with God through our Lord Jesus Christ. We have also obtained access through Him by faith into this grace in which we stand, and we rejoice in the hope of the glory of God. And not only that, but we also rejoice in our afflictions, because we know that affliction produces endurance, endurance produces proven character, and proven character produces hope. This hope will not disappoint us, because God's love has been poured out in our hearts through the Holy Spirit who was given to us. (Romans 5:1-5)

My son died because of a lie.

We had planned to go on a family vacation with another couple when the man fell sick. After being told by his doctor not to be around children, the man lied to us and said the doctor told him it was not contagious, so we could still come on the trip. As a result, my youngest son, Cody, caught the illness, causing a firestorm in his immune system. He developed a degenerative neurological disorder that ultimately claimed his life at age 17.

Despite his affliction, Cody was the most peaceful, joyous, and faith-filled young man I have ever met. Through faith, Cody truly believed he could "do all things through Him who strengthens" (Philippians 4:13).

The most joyous and peaceful people are often not those who have experienced little difficulty. Ironically, people whose lives have been relatively easy are often quite dissatisfied, feeling quickly overwhelmed, with a tendency to give up easily, and feeling entitled to an easy road. These people often do not know how to cope or respond when difficulties arise, and consistently seek comfort and safety instead of righteousness and truth. But eventually, difficulty will arise for everyone. In fact, we are promised by Jesus that we "will have suffering in this world" (John 16:33).

Rather than avoiding or ignoring difficulties, joyous and peaceful people are those who, like Cody, persevere in the face of affliction and walk through struggles to the end with Jesus. As Paul teaches in Romans 5:1-5, "Therefore, since we have been declared righteous by faith, we have peace with God through our Lord Jesus Christ. We have also obtained access through Him by faith into this grace in which we stand, and we rejoice in the hope of the glory of God. And not only that, but we also rejoice in our afflictions, because we know that affliction produces endurance, endurance produces proven character, and proven character produces hope. This hope will not disappoint us, because God's love has been poured out in our hearts through the Holy Spirit who was given to us".

My husband and I also walked through Cody's affliction, knowing full well the illness would ultimately take his life. Through faith, we sat beside him in countless PICU's. Through faith, we survived on four hours sleep or less each night so one of us could keep watch over him as he slept. Through faith, we stood by his bed, holding his hand as he took his last breath. I can honestly say, if not for Jesus walking with me, and most often carrying me, through these experiences, I would never have made it.

Yet, our hope did not disappoint us, because God's love sustained us through the pain, and we enjoyed 17 years of indescribable joy sharing Cody's life with him. We could've chosen powerlessness, blame, hopelessness, and despair, but Cody's perseverance inspired us and his faith and relationship with Jesus taught us to "run with endurance the race that lies before us, keeping our eyes on Jesus, the source and perfecter of our faith" (Hebrews 12:1-2). We discovered, like Cody, we are not victims, that we can endure more than we first believed, and that we are capable of more than we realize. As Paul said, we had God's peace through faith, and as a result, perseverance produced proven character in us; in other words, inner strength, endurance, and the ability to stand and face adversity, with hope and joy as the results.

What are some examples in your life where God has redeemed your suffering by producing perseverance, character, and hope in your life?

_____

_____

_____

How can your faith and your relationship with Jesus Christ carry you through times of adversity in the future?

_____

_____

_____

Prayer

Lord Jesus, I invite You to walk with me each and every moment of my day, and to carry me in Your arms when I am facing affliction, suffering, or difficulty. Love me through my pain, Jesus. Please strengthen me for the battle, producing perseverance, character, and hope in me as You develop my faith.

_____

Dr. Donna E. Lane (Ph.D.) is an author, university professor of counseling, and Christian counselor. She has written and presented at local, regional, national, and international conferences on such topics as trauma, grief and loss, Christian marriage, Christian parenting, and more. Donna has been married to David Lane since 1979, and they have three children: Hayden, Lindsey, Cody (who passed away in 2007), and two grandchildren, Coen and Petra.

Connect with Donna at http://www.doctordlane.com

Day 21
Healing Faith

My soul, praise Yahweh, and all that is within me, praise His holy name. My soul, praise the LORD, and do not forget all His benefits. He forgives all your sin; He heals all your diseases. He redeems your life from the Pit; He crowns you with faithful love and compassion. He satisfies you with goodness; your youth is renewed like the eagle. (Psalm 103:1-5)

In the spring of 2005, my husband was diagnosed with Stage 4 throat cancer. I was out of town for work the day he received the diagnosis and upon my return home, I found him singing and praising the Lord. Upon hearing the news, he called our pastor and was able to talk and pray with him and his wife, who was a cancer survivor. From that phone call and subsequent prayer, my husband had received hope for his burdened heart. He was convinced he would be healed. He was soon placed on many prayer chains, with the intercessors praying for his healing.

At the time of his diagnosis, we were reading through the Bible in a One-Year format. It is no coincidence that Psalm 103 was the Psalm we read the day Tim got the call that the biopsy was malignant. We clung to this promise from God's Word, that despite needing surgery to remove the cancer, Tim would be healed. Jesus used our confidence in Him to witness to our surgeon, oncologists, families, and co-workers.

Years later, we would again cling to this Psalm and its promises. I had broken my neck and had suffered a spinal cord injury resulting in paralysis from my shoulders down. The words and promises in this Psalm sustained me during dark nights as I lay in the ICU, as well as granting me the courage to boldly proclaim that I would walk out of the hospital fully functioning. I too, was placed on many prayer chains for my healing and recovery.

Our Lord Jesus is our Great Physician. He heals in many ways – sometimes instantaneously and other times He uses many hands and various methods to accomplish His healing in our bodies. Our LORD heals as a result of prayers, He heals when we show faith, He heals when we believe. For my husband and me, the Lord Jesus healed us not only as a result of our faith and the prayers of others, but also by using the skills granted by Him to our medical teams.

There are many instances in the Gospels of Jesus healing. All of these healings took place because people believed Jesus could and would heal them. These people include the Centurion who asked for healing of his servant, the paralytic who was lowered through the roof by his friends, the woman with the issue of blood, and the ten lepers. Then there was the blind beggar, Bartimaeus, who cried out to the Son of David for mercy. When asked what he wanted, Bartimaeus replied he wanted to see. "Go your way," Jesus told him. "Your faith has healed you." (Mark 10:52a)

Illness and accidents happen daily to believers as well as non-believers. Hope can and will sustain us through these tragic times. The Word tells us "Now without faith, it is impossible to please God" (Hebrews 11:6a). Job had faith, yet he had to endure tragedy, suffering, and loss before being restored by the LORD.

Had Jesus not healed us, I am not sure where our faith would be today. I can only believe we would still be rejoicing in His goodness and mercy. We only know His mercy to us was great, and we are humbly grateful. We know of faithful believers who have prayed as we did, only to lose the battle to a disease or to not regain the use of limbs. We don't understand why; we only know His ways are higher than our ways. He is God, I am not.

Do you believe Jesus still heals today? Why do you believe this?

_____

_____

_____

Have you prayed or known anyone who has prayed for healing and not received healing? How did you or they feel?

_____

_____

_____

Prayer

Lord Jesus, I do not understand Your mighty Ways and because of that, I have faith and believe You know what is best in our lives. May I continue to rejoice and have faith in You, when You heal and when You choose not to.

_____

Pam DePuydt is a retired banker and budding writer. She has been a Christ-follower for over 45 years, a Precept Bible leader and continues to be student of the Word.

Connect with Pam at https://www.facebook.com/pam.depuydt

Day 22
Day One

Not that I have already reached the goal or am already fully mature, but I make every effort to take hold of it because I also have been taken hold of by Christ Jesus. Brothers, I do not consider myself to have taken hold of it. But one thing I do: Forgetting what is behind and reaching forward to what is ahead, I pursue as my goal the prize promised by God's heavenly call in Christ Jesus. (Philippians 3:12-14)

My five-year-old son Caleb recently joined a flag football team. I did not attend my son's first day of practice, but I heard all about it from my husband. I learned from my husband that my son wanted to quit the team after the first day because his teammates were faster than him. I wanted to get to the bottom of this so I asked my son about his first day on the team. "Mommy, I don't want to play anymore. I'm not good. All the other kids are faster than me!" I tried not to chuckle as I explained to my son that he shouldn't be so hard on himself. "You can't compare your day one to their day twenty," I told him. I want to use this same sentiment to encourage anyone reading this devotional.

Many of us set out to accomplish goals and pursue dreams and get a feeling of defeat within the first year. Don't be discouraged! It's just your "day one!" I think about the passage in Philippians 3:12-14.The Apostle Paul displayed more maturity than my five-year-old son, obviously, but if we're honest, many of us struggle with persevering through challenging times.

My son assumed that his first day was everyone's first day! He did not realize that his new teammates had been practicing all summer long, training, gaining momentum, and endurance. My son also could not accept that anyone was faster than him because he had never seen it. He did not realize that during practice the kids playing offense or defense at any given moment were not his opponents, but his teammates! It reminds me of what Paul says in Romans 8:28, "We know that all things work together for the good of those who love God: those who are called according to His purpose." My son couldn't see how his teammates out running him or even tackling him was working for his good. You may not see the roadblocks and obstacles you're facing as good either. In the end, we all have that "Aha" moment when we realize that the opposition was actually pushing us towards our goal.

Paul's humility is commendable. He had every right to call himself mature, but chose the latter. Even though he was highly educated, well versed, and had studied under the most prestigious teachers of his time, he still remained in a continuous state of learning as demonstrated in Philippians 3:12, "Not that I have already reached the goal or am already mature."

I encourage you to set aside some quiet time to take in everything we've discussed here. Journal the good, the bad, the ups, and the downs as it relates to the amount of perseverance you've displayed throughout your journey. Try your best to see how each set back or tough time you endured has really been the ammunition that will catapult you into your destiny!

What goal(s) are you trying to reach that you haven't obtained yet?

_____

_____

_____

What are some of your frustrations in trying to reach your goal(s)? Write down 3-5 identifiable roadblocks you've encountered and 3-5 measurable steps towards reaching your goals?

_____

_____

_____

Prayer

Heavenly Father, I pray that You be involved in my pursuits and that You give me the strength to endure day one, month one, and even year one. Help me not to rush Your process for my life, and most of all Lord, let Your will be done. Help me to press towards the mark of the high calling in Your Son, Jesus, just like the Apostle Paul. I don't want to get ahead of myself. Even when I think I've arrived in my mind, help me to remain humble and persevere through the tough times that often come with pursuing purpose in You.

Fiona "Fee" Williams is a devoted wife and mother based out of Tampa, FL. She is a songwriter and blogger. In her music and writing, Fee wittingly shares learning moments from her life and expresses love and devotion to Jesus Christ. She and her husband write music and minister in song in the Tampa Bay Area. Fee is also a dynamic speaker and has used her gifts at several women's conferences in Tampa.

Connect with Fee at www.mrswilliamsspeaks.wordpress.com

Day 23
Temporary Pain, Eternal Glory

For I consider that the sufferings of this present time are not worth comparing with the glory that is going to be revealed to us. (Romans 8:18)

I remember the day my new bride of six months met me at the door with a smile on her face that was as radiant and beautiful as I had ever seen. "You're going to be a dad," she said.

The next 9 months flew by, and it was time for our firstborn to arrive.

She was almost ready to start pushing, when a nurse came in and broke her water. All of a sudden panic set in on the nurse's face, and she told me to go call the doctor. I did. They rushed in, took her out of the room, and into emergency surgery. The monitors were going wild and the nurse told me the baby's cord had prolapsed and his oxygen and blood flow was being cut off. They took her into a room and made me stay outside. I was afraid. My heart was hurting as I thought what might happen to our baby and my wife. Five minutes seemed like hours and finally the nurses rolled the baby bed out, and I was able to kiss my baby boy for the first time. He was beautiful and healthy, and I was praising God.

But my wife was still not there. I asked the nurses if she was okay, and there was silence as they walked away. After 30 minutes they called for me, opened the door, and rolled my wife out. I kissed her head and told her how beautiful our baby was. They wheeled her away to recovery and after two long hours my pain was over as we were together as a family. However, my wife's pain would continue for four to six more weeks. She had been cut open nearly in half to save our child. The pain was real. Excruciating, agonizing.

Six years and two more C-sections later we have three handsome boys. Two years have passed since the last time she felt that pain, and as I sit and watch her read to them and love them unconditionally I see the beauty of this passage and hear it expressed as she tells me, "I would do it 100 more times to be able to hold our children." The pain can't compare to the joy. The pain was temporary but the joy will last a lifetime.

In life we have troubles. We have pain and brokenness. We shed tears and ask, "Why" in the tough times, but if we know God and how good and loving He is, we can rejoice in those difficulties knowing that He works all things together for the good of those who love Him and are called according to His purpose. We can trust that this Word is true because He has allowed us to experience it in life, and we can certainly trust He will do it again.

If you are going through a difficult time now, I encourage you to trust this Word. Whatever the pain and circumstance, just read this Word out loud and ask God to give you the faith to believe it. If you are in Christ, nothing you go through is meaningless. Every pain, every heartache, every seemingly bad circumstance, it is all for your good and God's glory. I want you to know He hears you and loves you and promises to give the Holy Spirit to those who ask. Believe that God is who He says He is, will do what He says He will do, and that His Word is true for our lives.

Have you ever been or are you currently going through a trial that seems painful and meaningless?

_____

_____

_____

Think about the past trials you have endured. Did God keep His promises, and can you see how He turned the brokenness into beauty in your life? Praise Him for that today.

_____

_____

_____

Prayer

Father we love You and thank You for sending Jesus to take our place on the cross so we can come to You. We ask for the Holy Spirit to fill us and give us strength and wisdom and kindness and love. We need You to keep us near and let us dwell in your presence where peace and joy are found. You are worthy of all we endure, and we know You are working it out for our good. Help us to trust Your Word. In Jesus' name, Amen.

Josh Phillips is a child of God, the husband of my best friend and a dad to three awesome little boys. As a family we passionately seek to follow Jesus and make His name known among the nations.

Connect with Josh at http://Phillipspartyof5.wordpress.com

Day 24
Growing Weary in the Wait?

But those who trust in the Lord will renew their strength; they will soar on wings like eagles; they will run and not grow weary; they will walk and not faint. (Isaiah 40:31)

I'm not complaining, but there's a conflict in my life that God has yet to resolve after more than a decade of prayers. Well, several conflicts really. But there's one that rises to the top, and my attention is drawn to it time after time.

Things will even start to look promising, and I will pray, "Lord, is this it? Is this when You are going to answer my long-sought-after request?" But then what seems like a door opening is actually that same door slamming shut. It is then that I realize I must go back to God's waiting room to wait on and trust Him longer and more fiercely. Even though it hurts to head back to the waiting room, it would hurt me more to not experience these tests that stretch my faith.

Interestingly, the word "trust" here in Isaiah 40:31 is more accurately translated to "wait" on the Lord. I believe that's because it is in the waiting that our trust is deepened and faith is stretched. Our faith grows most when we can do nothing else but pray and wait patiently for God to respond and act on our behalf.

Ironically, Isaiah began by focusing on soaring before running and walking. Maybe that is because he was pointing to those lovely mountaintop moments, when God answers swiftly and clearly. It is then that we get to soar like an eagle—gaining a bird's-eye view of God's magnificent sovereignty and plan in our lives. I've experienced soaring a few times in my lifetime. But more often than not, my experiences typically involve trusting God by doing the two slower options.

Did you know that there's a difference between growing weary and not fainting? The Hebrew word for "weary" involves growing tired because of the harshness of life. But the Hebrew word for "faint" has more to do with losing motivation and power to move forward in our own human abilities. Both showcase commonplace experiences as faith-stretching opportunities.

God wants to use and redeem every harsh trial, unfair circumstance, and unrelenting problem to stretch your faith. What are some ways God might want you to stretch and trust Him more in a particular difficulty you are facing?

_____

_____

_____

Whenever we grow faint or weak, God gives us yet another avenue to deepen our trust by looking to Him for His strength to make it through every difficulty. In what areas are you running ahead or lagging behind the Lord? What do you need to do to stay more in step with Him as the pace setter of your race?

_____

_____

_____

Prayer

Father, what a privilege it is to know that Your power enables me to soar, run, and walk out my faith each day. Strengthen my ability to persevere during this time of difficulty, darkness, and weakness. For I know that what You are doing to strengthen me and my faith is far more important than any answer I might seek. In Jesus' name, Amen.

Beth Steffaniak is a life-coach and Christian blogger who is passionate about trusting God's redemption in all matters of life, but in particular the messes of marriage. She and her pastor husband enjoy spending as much free time as possible with their three adult sons and one daughter-in-law.

Connect with Beth at http://messymarriage.com/

Day 25
Persevering in Purity

"When the Lord saw that man's wickedness was widespread on the earth and that every scheme his mind thought of was nothing but evil all the time, the Lord regretted that He had made man on the earth, and He was grieved in His heart. (Genesis 6:5-6)

My 13 year old daughter schooled me. I didn't expect it. I didn't ask for it. But that's what happened. One summer evening my family selected a film for movie night from an online streaming service, and God taught me a lesson. And He used my little girl to do it.

Here's the low-down. The plot of the film we chose centered on a country singer who fell in love and married; then he skyrocketed to fame when a song he wrote for his wife caught fire. As he and his music grew in popularity, the sweet story turned sinister. He spent more and more time on the road away from his wife and young child, and as it turns out, absence didn't make his heart grow fonder. The more he distanced himself, the more he exposed himself to booze and drugs. He sank deeper and deeper into this lifestyle until a drunken night led to infidelity. That infidelity eventually advanced to a full-blown affair.

Having seen similar movies a time or two, I knew this character would eventually come to his senses and return to his "roots" of God and family. But my daughter, either unsure of the outcome or unwilling to experience the heartache the film caused her, ran from the room crying each time the singer strapped on a new sin habit. Several times my husband and I paused the movie to coax her back out to join us again with promises of coming redemption in the storyline.

It wasn't an easy sell to get her to finish watching the show with us. Through tears and anger she told us repeatedly, "I HATE this!" as she watched the family man turn his back on his family, dissolve his faith and obliterate his resolve.

In those moments I admired the tender, uncalloused heart beating in the chest of my last-born. At the ripe old age of plenty-nine, I've seen too much and heard too much to be so broken over sin. At least I told myself that lie. But the truth is, I want to be more like my daughter. And I don't think it's too late for me. I think I just need to spend MORE time with God (prayer, praise, Bible reading, and meditation) in Kingdom pursuits and LESS time consuming what the world has to offer. Cynicism and hard-heartedness make poor servants of our heavenly Father. I believe God is revealing that, for me, a sifting is in order. What about for you?

"Finally, brothers, whatever is true, whatever is honorable, whatever is just, whatever is pure, whatever is lovely, whatever is commendable – if there is any moral excellence and if there is any praise – dwell on these things" (Philippians 4:8).

Is a purge of your consumption in order? Are you filling your mind with movies, books, podcasts, music, or other things that could be desensitizing you to sin and its destructive power?

_____

_____

_____

Do you need to repent of any unconfessed sin in your own life to restore you to right standing with God?

_____

_____

_____

Prayer

Father, thank You for the example of childlike faith and purity. Give us the strength to make hard decisions in this sin-saturated world. Guide us toward pursuits that honor You and bring You glory and away from those with no redeeming value. Help us to persevere in purity and sanctify us toward ever-increasing holiness.

Lauren Sparks is a wife and mom to two daughters – one with special needs. She lives, worships Jesus, and teaches yoga in the Dallas, Texas area. She shares her adventures, victories, and flub-ups from her laptop.

Connect with Lauren at http://laurensparks.net

Day 26
Hope to Persevere

Therefore we do not give up. Even though our outer person is being destroyed, our inner person is being renewed day by day. (2 Corinthians 4:16)

After reading this verse I began to wonder, what is the definition of persevere, because that's what Paul is saying here, right? They persevered.

The dictionary says the following about the word persevere: *To persist a state, enterprise, or undertaking in spite of counter influences, opposition, or discouragement.*

I like the words "in spite of." As Christians, I think we hope for an easy path. We hope we won't face too many difficulties along the way. We hope that if we do, they won't be too unmanageable. And we hope that no matter what, it just works out in our favor.

We don't necessarily hope to have to persevere, because that would mean facing opposition. Many of our prayers sound something like this, "God, please bless me and keep me safe. Please let my day go smoothly, and let the work day go by quick and efficiently, and the afternoon of rest go by slow. Oh, but whatever will glorify and honor You, I want most importantly."

Is there anything wrong with wanting an easy day? Not at all. I hardly think God wants us to ask for problems. Why would He want that? But when it comes to His will, I believe God wants us to want whatever that looks like in our days. Sometimes that looks like opposition rather than ease. And no, we don't hope for that. We avoid that actually.

Paul, as he so often does, provides a silver lining to opposition. He more or less says that although our bodies are being destroyed, although we are facing affliction, although it's not all good, we are still okay. Although it doesn't look good, we persevere. Although we look bad on the outside, on the inside we're renewed. We get something in us that the world and an easy road wouldn't have been able to give to us.

In other words, when we have to persevere, we get to see God work in our lives. We get to depend on God, and we get to know that an incomparable weight of glory is being produced eternally. After all, that is what this life is supposed to be about, right? It's supposed to be about us getting others and ourselves ready for eternity.

So, let's agree to persevere. I'm not saying let's hope for the worst, but I'm saying let's trust God whatever happens today. Let's trust God will make a way, whether it's easy or hard, because if you have to persevere, you get to lean on God. What could be better than learning how to lean and depend on the Lord?

Are you happier with coasting through and thanking God, or with trusting Him to bring the best out of the worst?

_____

_____

_____

What if we all chose the road of perseverance because of the glory we could give God afterwards?

_____

_____

_____

Prayer

God, thank You for Your perfection. Thank You that in the bad, You bring out the best. Help us to persevere during those less than ideal times and to know that there is much glory to be had to honor Your name in those moments. In Jesus' name, Amen.

Chanel Moore is an author, blogger, and co-founder of Chosen Designs Online. She currently produces a series of weekly minute devotions on her website and social media pages.

Connect with Chanel at www.noworneverbetter.com

Day 27
The Most Dangerous
Temptation

Therefore, since we have a great high priest who has passed through the heavens—Jesus the Son of God—let us hold fast to the confession. For we do not have a high priest who is unable to sympathize with our weaknesses, but One who has been tested in every way as we are, yet without sin. Therefore let us approach the throne of grace with boldness, so that we may receive mercy and find grace to help us at the proper time. (Hebrews 4:14-16)

I never played sports in high school, but I was part of the high school drill team. One requirement was to be able to stand at attention, sometimes for long periods of time in all kinds of weather. We typically had to stand at attention at the beginning and end of the band performances at football and basketball games and also at band competitions. It was a physically and mentally challenging experience. Fortunately, because I never gave up, I earned my varsity letters in drill team for all four years of high school. This experience was only a small life lesson in perseverance, nothing in comparison to what Jesus endured.

During His time on earth, Jesus experienced life's everyday temptations. Just like us, He was tempted to lie, be angry and impatient, or give in to His fears. Fortunately for us, Jesus never gave in to sin. His perseverance in the face of temptation and His death on the cross won our salvation. When we admit that we need a Savior and believe in our heart that God raised Jesus from the dead, we are saved. (Romans 10:9)

Because of this, as Christians we can always draw near to God with a confident assurance that we will receive all the mercy and help we need to persevere in our own fight against temptations and sin. God calls us His children, and just like an earthly father will do everything he can to protect and help his kids, God wants to help us resist in the face of our everyday temptations.

Of course, we might be tempted to fight in our own strength. In Thomas Wilson's, *Maxims of Piety and Christianity*, p.151, he says, "The most dangerous of all temptations is to believe that one can avoid or overcome them by our own strength, and without asking the help of God."

We humans tend to rely on own strength and effort. We call it being independent, but we should probably call it "not smart." It's easy to forget that Jesus not only understands what it's like to live on this earth, but He has abundant grace and mercy stored up to help us in our daily struggles.

Today, let's remember to look to Jesus for help, rather than to ourselves, in our persevering fight against sin and temptation.

What is one temptation you face that you're prone to fight in your own strength?

_____

_____

_____

How does it help you to know that Jesus was tempted in every respect as you are but never sinned?

_____

_____

_____

Prayer

Thank You, Jesus, for Your life, death, and resurrection that won our salvation. Thank You also for Your mercy and grace stored up for us for today. Help us to look to You for the persevering strength we need in our fight against sin and temptations.

Jennifer Hinders is a freelance writer and blogger. Her writings are inspired from her own life experiences: her faith, raising children, owning a dog, and her family.

Connect with Jennifer at https://www.jhinders.com

Day 28
Labor Pains

When a woman is in labor she has pain because her time has come. But when she has given birth to a child, she no longer remembers the suffering because of the joy that a person has been born into the world. So you also have sorrow now. But I will see you again. Your hearts will rejoice, and no one will rob you of your joy. (John 16:21-22)

My mom was by my side during the birth of each of my children. "Don't tense up," she reminded me as I labored. "You don't want to work against your body."

Amid the excruciating pain, I imagined myself breathing into the contractions. I tried to embrace the struggle knowing the outcome was meeting my baby. During the pain of labor, God gently reminded me how pain serves a purpose. And when we entrust our pain into His care, the result is remarkable. God makes beauty out of ashes.

Today, I encourage you to lean into the ache of your circumstances like you might lean into labor pains. Don't work against the pain. Ask God for His outcome and trust His sovereignty. Declare hope and confidence over your hurts. Be confident "...that He who started a good work in you will carry it on to completion until the day of Christ Jesus" (Philippians 1:6). We can rest assured knowing God honors obedience.

The Christian walk is not an easy one. It's filled with painful times, which eventually produce good outcomes. But your labor is not in vain. Your pain is not in vain. Although we struggle through uncomfortable and even excruciating situations here on earth, we can stand firm, in His unwavering goodness. "Therefore, my dear brothers, be steadfast, immovable, always excelling in the Lord's work, knowing that your labor in the

Lord is not in vain" (1 Corinthians 15:58).

The truth is nothing is wasted here on earth. No circumstance, painful moment, or bad memory is purposeless. God turns each and every situation into an opportunity to further his Kingdom. He will use it all for His glory.

A woman in labor relies heavily on endurance and her mindset. The Christian walk also requires much perseverance and training of the mind. It is in labor that we truly must keep our thoughts on the prize, the end goal. Similarly, our lives require us to continually meditate on the characteristics of our loving Father in heaven. It requires a lot of trust to truly believe that the pain we suffer here on earth serves a specific purpose.

In Him, we have peace despite our circumstances. In Him, we have hope despite what the world tells us. "I have told you these things so that in Me you may have peace. You will have suffering in this world. Be courageous! I have conquered the world" (John 16:33).

Try to imagine your life as a woman in labor. The time will come when the pain has served its purpose and joy ensues. How would your mindset change if you knew that all your pain was serving a purpose, a greater outcome?

_____

_____

_____

What Scripture verses can you claim for yourself to encourage you to look at the bigger picture?

_____

_____

_____

Prayer

Lord God, I know everything has a time, purpose, and season. Help me withstand the circumstances, look to You, and have the endurance to continue when it's hard. Help me realize that indeed my labor is not in vain.

Mikella Van Dyke is a dancer, writer, and business owner who lives in a small town in New Hampshire. Mikella grew up in Thailand as a missionary kid which has left her with a deep love of Thai culture, Thai food, her rice-cooker, and mangos. Mikella is passionate about God's Word. You can find her writing on her blog, Instagram, and Facebook about God, family, and business.

Connect with Mikella at www.chasingsacred.com

Day 29
Persevering Through Grief

Therefore, brothers, by the mercies of God, I urge you to present your bodies as a living sacrifice, holy and pleasing to God; this is your spiritual worship. Do not be conformed to this age, but be transformed by the renewing of your mind, so that you may discern what is the good, pleasing, and perfect will of God. (Romans 12:1-2)

"Honey," my mom would say, "don't stare. That's not polite. No, don't point, either." But when I was a kid, I couldn't look away from a child in a wheelchair. We were all trained as children to politely look the other way when we passed by someone with special needs.

This is life for us now. My daughter was nineteen and single when she gave birth to perfectly healthy Allie. All our lives were suddenly overwhelmed the day Allie received a brain injury when she was ten months old. She was shaken and suffocated by a babysitter who was watching her when my daughter was at work. Allie was in a coma for ten days. She emerged from that coma severely disabled with cerebral palsy and quadriplegia.

We knew we'd never get our lives back the moment we walked into the hospital room and saw Allie motionless in the bed. Her tiny body was swaddled from head to toe in bandages with wires and nodes attached to her head in a mass of tangled hair and gauze. A giant machine stretched its tentacles into her mouth and nostrils mechanically pushing oxygen into her lungs, and then an electronic trigger suddenly reversed the airflow and carbon dioxide wooshed out in a robotic exhale. Puuuush. Woooosh. Puuuush. Woooosh. It was surreal, devastating. It was the first day of our new normal.

Grief is where our lives were headed. This word "grief" is derived from an old French verb "grever." It could also be translated "to burden." A character in the Charles Dickens novel *Great Expectations* said, "Grief unmakes the griever's world." To the ones grieving, there's a sense of exclusion from the world. The world passes by in slow motion, and the griever wonders, "Are they oblivious, or am I?"

Grieving loss implies that somehow, deep within you, you're looking for something you'll never have again.

After eight weeks, Allie was stable enough to leave the hospital. As a single mother, our young daughter was not able to care for Allie. My wife and I could not fathom the thought of our granddaughter going into foster care in her condition. We did what we thought anyone would do: we adopted Allie and became the parents of a severely disabled little girl. This did not relieve our grief. It complicated it.

I had followed Jesus for more than twenty years when this happened, but my theology quit working. John 15 came to mind: "No longer do I call you servants, for the servant does not know what his master is doing; but I have called you friends." I wondered where my friend Jesus went. I couldn't believe He could let this horrific thing happen to me, to us, to Allie. He had the ability to help, but didn't. That's the theological conclusion I came to. He stood on the sidelines and watched.

But I couldn't leave it there. I don't think the Holy Spirit would let me. I rehearsed this mantra, "God is good all the time. All the time God is good." This is an African American spiritual proverb birthed in suffering and oppression.

One translation of the above verses is, "...don't let yourselves be squeezed into the shape dictated by this present age" (NTE). In this present age, there is grief. In the age to come, every tear is wiped away. We have great hope. New Testament theologian N.T. Wright often asks, "How would you live if God were running the show?" Whether we can wrap our minds around it or not, God is running the show. So what's the application? Start living like it. Live like God is running things in your life.

The key is transforming the mind. This is something we have a very difficult time with. We think we can muscle our way through a few behavioral adjustments, self-help style. Instead of sacrificing self as the verse exhorts, we take an approach that attempts to preserve self.

A transformed mind is contained within a life of self-sacrifice. The two are conjoined twins. A transformed mind happens when the human will merges with the Living Spirit of God. It is through a transformed mind that hope, faith, and joy begin to invade your life and overflow into the lives around you.

Having a transformed mind gives the believer new sight. We began to see that some of our struggles are actually gifts. Allie is the greatest gift we've ever been given. Her life brings joy and love we never knew we could have. Her laughter is infectious. She is who God made her to be. Yes, she's broken. But who isn't?

What or who is God sending into your world of grief? He wants to do something within you that you never thought possible. Grief stretches our capacity to contain, enjoy, and be distributors of love. Love is present in grief.

How did God bring you through the most difficult season of your life? Make a list of the things you are thankful for that came out of that season.

_____

_____

_____

Who do you know that is grieving right now? What could you do to help shoulder the burden he or she is carrying in this time of personal isolation?

_____

_____

_____

Prayer

Father, love isn't simply one of Your attributes. Your Word says that, "God is love" (1 John 4:8). Father, we simply ask that as You walk with us through our deepest seasons of suffering and sadness, that You infuse us with the ability to love You and love others. Help us understand that this is how You heal us.

Bryon Mondok is a digital engagement practitioner, mission's pastor, and former missionary. He loves to read, write, and run.

Connect with Bryon at bryon.mondok@gmail.com

Day 30
Remedy for Spiritual Depression

He asked him the third time, "Simon, son of John, do you love Me?" Peter was grieved that He asked him the third time, "Do you love Me?" He said, "Lord, You know everything! You know that I love You." "Feed My sheep," Jesus said. (John 21:17)

Peter had failed. He had fallen. He had flat out denied the Lord, not once, not twice, but three times! After arrogantly claiming that he would never deny the Lord, even if all the other disciples did, Peter did just that, and thus proved why arrogance is so foolish. At this point in the story, Peter had repented, but he was far from experiencing total victory. The fight against your failure is never a first round knockout. The race to recover, especially from such a humbling failure, isn't a sprint, it's a marathon. If you've majorly blown it, you know the battle Peter was in. It's in that mental battle where you recognize you're redeemed, but you are still struggling with shame and disappointment in yourself. You know the right things, but you feel so wrong.

Recovering from these battles can be difficult. If we're not careful, we can slip into a chronic state of spiritual depression. We can drift into a perpetual path of painful inner struggle. How do we avoid this painful and problematic condition? I would suggest that we conquer this beast the same way Peter did: with Jesus' help.

Jesus asked Peter some difficult, hard hitting questions, and then gave him some practical commands. He asked Peter if he loved Him. He had to unfortunately and uncomfortably ask this of Peter three times. Three opportunities to publicly affirm Him after publicly denying

Him three times. How gracious is our Lord? We'll leave this aspect of the scene alone for the time being, but I definitely encourage you to reflect on this particular point privately. Continuing on, we see that Peter responded humbly three times. The questions were challenging and the commands were practical, and it's in both that we find the answer to our problem with spiritual depression. Peter was able to get out of the slough of despondency because Jesus brought him back to the basics. Jesus firmly placed Peter's feet on a reliable foundation. What were the reliable and foundational basics? To love Jesus and serve others.

My friends, it's that simple. If you are going through a season of spiritual depression that has been birthed from your failure, I urge you to return to the basics. Live a life of love with the Lord and humbly serve others. Your condition doesn't have to be chronic if you are listening to the Great Physician and following His spiritual prescription.

What areas of your spiritual walk have you over complicated or neglected?

_____

_____

_____

What is a very real and practical way you can serve others in your world?

_____

_____

_____

Prayer

Lord, if I have drifted from You, please bring me back to the basics in our relationship. Help me have a genuine and vibrant walk with You. I do love You, and I pray You help me serve others. In the powerful name of Jesus, Amen.

Eric Souza is a follower of Christ, who is married to his beautiful wife Betsy. They are blessed with three beautiful children. Eric is also the founding pastor of Reach Jacksonville, a Calvary

Chapel Church in Jacksonville, Florida. Through a simple, practical, and honest approach to Scripture, Eric has led many in verse by verse studies through several books of the Bible.

Connect with Eric at www.reachjax.com